The Power of Self

{Practical *Keys to reclaiming your true value*}

{Ones true value is determined by the source from which it
is created and manifested through the object of value
accepting and displaying the value that is placed upon it}

Gary L. Wilkerson 2013

God's purpose and perspective of (SELF) is for us to;

<u>Serve</u> — *the need of another*

<u>Empower</u> — *others to prosper*

<u>Love</u> — *others without applying special conditions*

<u>Foster</u> — *the growth and development of someone else's life*

The book and its author

by Gwendolyn Onuekusi – Spiritual Advisor/Servant Prayer Warrior

First I want to thank God for giving my brother Gary Wilkerson, the desire and anointing to write this book. It is truly a tool for character building in every aspect of our lives. As we read we will find areas of correction and moments of reflection to the things which we have learned in this book. I do know the author to be a man of integrity, and for the years that I have known him. He has proven to be a man of character, love, and understanding. He is always striving to be a good representative of God in everything that he can. This book is a must read and a must share for all. I highly recommend this book to ignite your faith, stir your spirit, and to destroy the works of the enemy that might be challenging your life.

The Power of Self

Cover Concept
by
Gary L. Wilkerson & Athanasia Drosostalista Boura

Cover Design & Graphics
by
Athanasia Drosostalista Boura

Table of Contents

Preface

From the time we are born life's journey has had its' way with us, eating away at the very substance of who and what we were created to be. Purpose for most by their adolescent years would have become but a distant shadow. What has happened is that the environment and the people which formed the habitat to which we would grow by had become dysfunctional to put it lightly. We grew up hearing statements being directed towards us that were designed to tear down and destroy. Even, if it was not the intention of the persons delivering them. Words are meant to be the building blocks of life and love the very foundation to which they are built upon. But the truth is very few people actually experience the privilege and benefit of having a life filled with positives. So what happens is we become a product of our environment and our mindset and behavior becomes the norm?

Because we live smack in the middle of the destruction that is wreaking havoc on our lives, we in most cases never give attention to it, not even realizing that there is an issue. Before you know it we have matured into products of the very environment to which we were exposed to, and now we are planting the same seed of destruction into the lives of others, even our children.

How can we change this, where is the chain to be broken? Is this what God intended when he created us in His image and likeness? Is this what He expected to see reflected as His image and likeness in the earth that He created for mankind? I say not, so is it possible to correct the damage that has been done from generation to generation? Is there an answer and if so, how do we begin to access it? *Where do we start?*

The discovery of the greatest power in existence is available to everyone. Whether you are a child, an adolescent, an adult, or a senior. This God given ability is accessible to you for good success in relationships of any kind. ***Practical keys to successful relationships by reclaiming your true value,*** Is a very simple process that will literally change the way to which you engage relationships with those in your life.

Pastoral Commentary

By Pastor William T. Rucker Jr.

"The Power of Self"

I'am so proud of you! Truly God is leading you to help change our thoughts, about what relationship is to be like. You are so thoughtful, it was a delight to see that each chapter jumped off the page. It was like reading with 3D glasses.

I was moved with emotion, seeing you put everything you had on the the line, regarding relationship. I absolutely agree with your concept of putting the family and the church on high alert, regarding the issue we face as a people.

What a great book! I feel like you were speaking to me personally...From the very first sentence I was hooked, and I couldn't put it down, as each chapter drew me deeper to give a spiritual and earthly examination on my relationships. I am sure that each reader will be be blessed. Quote;"This is a bible on relationships", and is really needed. Rev. Dr. P. M. Smith, would always say that "God is all about relationship or nothing at all."

I am grateful to you, for allowing God to know you, and not just use you. I'm going to read your masterpiece over and over again . The church, community, and nation needs to know God's purpose for us.

Thank you again for helping me heal.

Forward

By Andrew I Okoh Ph.D., MFT

The Power of Self

Those in the society who are a little bit advanced in age, still remember when telephone had "Party lines" and Television had knobs that you had to rotate to the left or to the right to tune to your desired channel. Net was either something women used to hold their hair in place, or an extensive instrument used by fishermen to catch a lot of fish at one time. Today we are so technologically advanced that we are able to achieve feats that were not even dreamed of in those days. We can attend meetings with people from all over the world without actually leaving our bedrooms. We boast of how many followers we have on Twitter and how many friends we have on Facebook and other social networks, without the slightest chance that we would ever meet some of these people physically. As good, and as useful as technology is, some of the side effects seem to be deeper isolation and alienation from each other. Even in our most intimate relationships, such as our marriages and families. There is no doubt that we are losing our sense of self while our relationships slip through our fingers. We still find ourselves feeling surprised, and horrified when we hear that a well-known and technologically well-connected individual committed suicide. In such cases we belch out the rhetoric question, "Why?" and top it with comment such as, "He/She had everything!"

The good news is that there is a solution to this malady. "For God so loved the world that He gave His only Begotten Son…" John 3:16. Our Creator who paid the ultimate price to redeem and restore us to a relationship with Him, who loves us. In the "Power of Self', Mr. Wilkerson takes the reader on a journey that begins within. It is a journey that goes back to the basics, from the Word of God. The "Power of Self' is about finding yourself, finding the value of your relationships and the power that keeps it alive in Christ Jesus.

ACKNOWLEDGEMENTS

I give honor to my precious Lord, the Most High God who blessed me with a mandate to pen this revealing literary piece, that many will be awakened to the reality of the God ordained value and purpose that was placed upon their lives. May He forever be glorified in the lives that are touched and changes by the revelations contained in this book.

To my dear precious wife, who without her in my life and all she brings to the table that enabled me to complete this auspicious task. I could never have completed this mission without her. She has labored with me in that she covered me and empowered me through constant intercession. She selflessly allowed me to minimize my time with her and forgo assignments she needed me to complete around the home, in order that I could give my time and focus to completing this project for the glory of God, so that it would be a blessing to the lives of those who read it.

I thank the many random people I encountered, who allowed me to bounce ideas off them and extract answers to the many questions I may have probed them for in my research.

A, very special thanks to my dearest sister Deborah Freeman, and my amazing daughter in-law Jamaica Murphy-Wilkerson, for their time and insight with aiding me in the editing of my manuscript through their excellence in proof reading.

To Athanasia Drosostalista Boura, a very gifted young lady, who allowed her hand to be guided by the hand of God in capturing the artistic vision I had in mind for this God inspired book.

To my dear friend Pastor William T. Rucker Jr., your words of support are all inspiring. Having you as a life friend from small boy's to mighty men of God, is so much more than we could have ever imagined. But, such is the way of our God, and together we shall continue to walk in the steps He has ordered. I am eternally grateful that we are on the winning team.

To my amazing friend. A man of God, who God miraculously brought into my life. Andrew I Okoh, Ph.D., MFT. Thank you for sharing your heart, your thought and your professional expertise in writing the forward to my book. I am forever grateful to have you and the witness of the selfless love that you express towards your people in Nigeria, that God has called you to.

Without the true to life testimonials that have been shared, this book would be incomplete in its relativity to how understanding value and purpose can effect positive change in peoples' lives. Thank all of you who revealed the blessing of selflessness in your lives with our readers. Continued blessings always.

Last but not least to all of the many readers who pick up this book, thank you! Use it as a tool to help you navigate your way to more successful relationships that shape the world around you in the fulfilling of your God ordained purpose. God Bless you!

Introduction;

"The Power of Self"; & discovering the key to successful relationships by reclaiming your true value. Is a master key that will unlock your insight and aid in you becoming and being the very best you possible. This guide will provide you with valuable information as to the *power* you hold which is deeply embedded within your will. You could even say that it is the driving force and true identity of your will. Without it you would actually have no will of your own.

This book is written to be a resource applicable to relationships of all types, and will guide you through having good success with any relationship that you might encounter. The success that you experience will be based upon your execution of your understanding to your value and purpose within the relationship.

Types of relationships to which you hold value and have purpose in are – parent/child, sibling, extended family, friends/associates, authorities/subordinates for example teacher/student, employer/employee etc., boyfriend/girlfriend, husband/wife. Note; all of the relationships mentioned in this book are a direct derivative of the Creator and His creation of the human kind. Whose value and purpose is predestined by God, but He has given us the ability to choose for ourselves what we desire. So then the thing to determine in this review is are you pouring into God's creation or taking away from it? Now that's something to think about. That is a question that the Creator Himself will ask of us some day.

Our Will; *is our mental ability to decide or choose for ourselves; a strong desire or determination. Housed within the chambers of*

our soul, is our mind which is the motherboard and distribution
center to the actions of our thoughts, and emotions.

What is value?

A noun; The regard that something is held to deserve; the importance to or preciousness of something. *Example;* "your support is of great value"

Definition – relative worth, merit, or importance. Importance / usefulness, quality, principles / beliefs.

God's purpose and perspective of (SELF) is for us to;

Serve – the need of another

Empower – others to prosper

Love – others without applying special conditions

Foster – the growth and development of someone else's life

SELF - is the driving force of one's Will, the place or element which determines how you choose to live your life. ***Your Will*** is the only thing under your complete control. Every other aspect and element of who you are in life is controlled from within your Will.

There are only two choices you have to select from, that will determine your effect on and your legacy to the world.

SELFLESSNESS - is determined and designed to consider others before one's self, and to give rather than receive. To, protect and provide. To, admonish and encourage. To help and sustain another, is its preference.

SELFISHNESS - is singleness of mind, body and soul, with a strong desire to only please or service its own needs and personal desire. It places itself above everything and everyone. Nothing or no one is more important.

Okay, now that we have a foundational understanding of our will and one's self. Let's begin our review with a very controversial statement.

God, the creator of all things, created man in His own likeness and image for His own pleasure. *Now it appears that God in His creation of man was being selfish, but that is so far from the truth as it relates to His intentions and He proves that by His actions that followed the creation.*

God created man this way and gave him his own kingdom to have authority and dominion. His purpose in doing so was to have something within His creation that He could personally relate to and recognize to be even as He is. But with that He also gave His creation all of the same attributes that He himself has. He gave them, creative authority, dominion authority, and the authority to determine for himself, how he would use his authority within his kingdom.

He, _mankind_ could choose to control and manipulate those in his kingdom life {_which is contrary to the dominion given_}, or he could choose to encourage and nurture them to the enhancement of his kingdom life by applying their God given ability to his for a stronger, more valuable purpose in his kingdom life and the Kingdom of God the creator.

Chapter I

Parent and Child Relationships

The relationship between parent and child is by far the most unique and often misunderstood of all relationships. I have found in my personal experience, as a parent, minister, and counselor. That one of the primary reasons these particular relationships often do not accomplish their designed purpose. Is that parents and children act outside of their roles in the relationship. The main reason for this is the lack of understanding in regards to what boundaries are and how they are to be imposed. A parent is supposed to usurp loving and nurturing authority over the child. This is how they will learn the way of a child, by what the parent teaches. So in essence the responsibility is the parents to direct the child in the way to which he/she is supposed to conduct themselves.

❧Respect must be earned not demanded☙

I believe that the approach to parenting is the main cause for the unwanted actions of the children. Parents for the most part will imposed their will on the child rather than simply teaching them what is the right and wrong way to behave. Respect must be earned not demanded. Using brute force will never accomplish the desired goal for a parent attempting to develop children into model citizens.

If a parent in their effort, would take the time to reveal to the child that they have choices, and that with each choice there is a consequence, or a benefit/reward. They would then have concrete information to evaluate how they should approach handling opportunities and encounters that are essential to developing character.

This is where the importance of knowing and understanding one's value and purpose, as it relates to the parent child relationship, will bring balance and stability to the relationship and family environment.

God in his love for us provided a detailed guide to how we are to conduct ourselves in relationships. He even used himself in many instances to show how what he has instituted in his word, is to be carried out by his children.

Pro 15:33 The fear of the LORD *is* the instruction of wisdom; and before honor *is* humility.

Honor and trust must be established before respect can be rewarded

Parents, in order to establish obedience in a child you must first be disciplined to conduct yourself in a manner that is honorable. **Honor** and **trust** must be established before respect can be earned and rewarded. Keep in mind that honor is often linked to humility, and one who is humble will always get the attention that respect demands. Remember your stature and size alone can be threatening to a child, add to that a loud and forceful character. You can almost guarantee that the child's response will result in being defensive and rebellious. It is a natural instinct driven by emotion. Sort of a protective device for the child who has no other means of conquering, what to them appears to be a threat to their safety.

What then is your value and purpose as a parent to your child or any child that might be in your care.

Value – a parents value to a child is in the selfless way you serve the child and reveal to them how they are valued in your sphere of life, and to their importance of contributing to the world and the lives of those around them.

Purpose – your purpose as a parent is to be a protector, a provider, a nurturer. Children must know that they can trust you to care for them and protect them. They must establish an awareness, that they have a need to honor you, and that need is long life according to God's word. That is a message of wisdom, that is to be shared with all children by their parents.

Deu 5:16 "Honor your father and your mother, just as the LORD your God commanded you, so that your life will be long and things will go well for you in the land that the LORD your God is giving you.

When, a child understands that they were created by God. And that they have a specific purpose in life, you can show them how that purpose begins with honoring their parents. They at that point now have a foundation to build their lives upon. You as the parent are responsible for providing them the building blocks of life, to begin the development of the glorious person that God intended them to be.

Consider what you desire your child to be, is it what God desires? The child's representation of your desire, will be a direct result of your teachings and exposure to life habits etc..

Pro 22:6 Train a child in the way appropriate for him, and when he becomes older, he will not turn from it.

God has provided a road map in His word. His instruction to all parents is simply train them according to His word, and it doesn't matter if you see signs of trouble. That child will always return to what has been instilled in them. Children will have periods in life to where they are not sure of what to do or which way they should go. But you are not to worry, because they have a foundation that's unshakable.

<u>Eph 6:4</u> Fathers, do not provoke your children to anger, but bring them up by training and instructing them about the Lord.

The instruction, not to provoke children is intended to address both parents. The emphasis is placed on the father because of his position as head of the family structure. When, the order of structure, as God has established, and ordained it to be, is misrepresented. This displacement of order, confuses the innate instinct of the child to obey. When a child and parent relationship is strained or out of order, it is always to the fault of the parent, not asserting their God given authority and responsibility to train the child according to God's word. Relationship is the result of two or more human beings engaging in interactions with each other for the purpose of cohabitation within a fixed environment. Neither of the individuals involved in cohabitation can succeed without the other. God designed the human to require certain elements to survival that can only come from another individual. What the other individual has to give provides nurturing to the mind, body, soul, and spirit of another. When this does not occur then that individual suffers, because what was designed to be received from another has been taken away by another.

Only a parent can give a child what it requires to develop and sustain a healthy life as a child. Only a child can give a parent what it requires to develop and sustain a healthy life as a parent. These requirements cannot be successfully fulfilled by any other individual or being, except God.

❧what we have belongs to someone else❧

The ability and qualities that an individual has, is not meant for that person to keep for their own self use. It is purposed for the use of someone else. You see what we have belongs to someone else. It comes down to what we will to do, as it relates to raising

our children. Thus we have to chose whether to be selfish or

selfless.

A Selfless Parent

- ➢ Considers, and gives to a child's every need, without giving way to the cost. It's worthy of the parents sacrifice for the child's sake.

- ➢ Sees the potential of the child and will forgo their own desire, in order to nurture the dreams of the child.

- ➢ Will protect and support the child throughout their childhood, and even into adulthood.

- ➢ Will delay their own dreams, in order to build upon the hopes of the child's future.

- ➢ Will always exercise integrity, when it concerns promises committed to the child.

- ➢ Always seeks and endeavors to restore a child when they have suffered loss or brokenness.

- ➢ Will never leave a child in disappointment or distrust.

A Selfish Parent

➤ Doesn't think that a child's need or desire should supersede theirs.

➤ Will avoid acknowledging a child's desire and even use the child to fulfill their own desire or dreams. Living their life through the child.

➤ Will leave a child exposed to harm from others, if the child threatens their livelihood or opportunity for success.

➤ Sees a child as having plenty of time to think about the future. So they will spend most of their time and efforts toward fulfilling their own future.

➤ Will lie to or about a child, if it benefits their agenda and purpose.

➤ Will accuse a child of hurting themselves, when making wrong or bad decisions to avoid fault.

➤ Has no issue with disappointing the child, if the requirement to the child's need is too costly or supersedes their own need.

Improving upon the way you do things is the first step to change

Now in considering the subject matter you have just read. Where do you fit in? What kind of parent have you been? Do you find that in some way you fit into any of these categories, or even may have done some of the things that are mentioned here? If you, some how found that you qualify, and by your own actions fall into the selfish category, and truthfully we all do in some way. That doesn't mean that you are not a good parent. It simply means that you can acknowledge your shortcomings, and that you could use some help towards change. Improving upon the way you do things is the first step to change after having acknowledged there is an issue. God said in His word that when you know the truth that you will be free from the bondage of selfishness. Reclaim your true value by seeking truth, through

spending time in God's word. His word will guide you in the way of

parenting, enabling you to establish a right relationship with your

children.

(ASV) Joh 8:32 and ye shall know the truth, and the truth shall make you free.

(ASV) Psa 119:105 **Nun.** Thy word is a lamp unto my feet, And light unto my path.

(ASV)Pro 6:23 For the commandment is a lamp; and the law is light; And reproofs of instruction are the way of life:

Chapter II

Sibling Relationships

❧The role of the parent continues in the sibling relationships❧

Sibling relationships are a direct spin off of parent/child relationships. The behavioral patterns which have been established in the parent/child relationships become evident within the sibling relationships.

Historically one of the most prevalent aspects of sibling relationships is sibling rivalry. Sibling rivalry is present as a result of the inability of and lack of knowledge on behalf of the parent to instill in the children, the value and importance of their own individuality in comparison to their sibling and within the family structure. The siblings and the parents must be sensitive to and acknowledge the unique individuality and personality of each sibling and how their character adds to and even completes the overall value of the family.

Sibling rivalry in most cases take on a negative value within the family structure, and the family is unfortunately deemed to be labeled as dysfunctional. However this does not necessarily have to be the case in your family. The personal ability and responsibility, of the parents to recognize and develop, the personalities of each sibling, will lead to, the building up, of their character that they complement each other.

Teaching a child early on in their development, that they and their sibling both have a very important role within the family structure, will enable them to develop their individuality, and feel secure knowing that they hold great value within the family structure. Becoming secure in themselves, they are then able to engage in intense fellowship without bringing destruction and dis-ease to the family. This is accomplished through the ability to forgive one another for any hurtful behavior inflicted upon each other during the intense fellowship (quarreling). Through forgiveness they also develop the ability to esteem the need of the other above their own.

❧Selflessness demands forgiveness❧

Selflessness demands that forgiveness be extended to a sibling whom you might be having intense fellowship with. Selflessness in this event is a character trait that says, even though you hurt me, I will not hold it against you, because you are important to me, and I need you in my life.

Sibling rivalry has been an issue within the family structure since the fall of man in the Garden of Eden. As a result of the fall God placed man outside of Eden for his own protection and for the preservation of that very sacred part of His creation we know to be eternity.

As with Cain and his brother Abel who both sought the favor of their earthly and especially their heavenly father. Their confrontation tragically ended in the taking of another's life. Many relationships today are destroyed by the misguided intentions of another. Instead, of Cain simply offering his very best as did his brother. He chose rather to envy his brothers offering and the favor given to him of the lord. So often our children are not made aware that their best is as good as the next persons, and that is all that is required of them, is to give their best in what they do.

(ISV) Gen 4:6 the LORD asked Cain, "Why are you so upset? Why are you depressed?
Gen 4:7 If you do what is appropriate, you'll be accepted, won't you? But if you don't do what is appropriate, sin is crouching near your doorway, turning toward you. However, you must take dominion over it."

Cain chose to ignore God's instruction to take dominion and instead gave way to anger and depression, which always leads to destructive behavior. He determined that his own self worth was more important than his brother and even God, his heavenly father.

The bible records numerous accounts of sibling rivalry. This has been a major issue throughout the existence of mankind. The bible made no attempt at all to cover up the dysfunctional behavior within the family structure. The bible actually shows accounts to the contrary to prove that healthy sibling relationships are possible. When, a family beginning with the parents, adhere to the guidelines referenced in the bible, parent/child and sibling relationships become a blessing for a lifetime.

Case and point, as with Jacob and Esau whose relationship could have ended tragically as did Cain and Able. But God's intervention unlike with Cain and Able did make a difference. Over time, a relationship that had been devastated, by favoritism and deceit instituted by their parents. Somehow did manage, to get back on track, regardless of the negative influence from the parents. The relationship was restored because they chose to follow God's instruction and apologized to one another and offered forgiveness.

❧Humility is the foundation to restoration❦

Jacob had stolen Esau's birth right, and in fear of what Esau would do fled on the instruction of his mother. He remained in hiding for years. However, due to the blessing which his father Isaac placed upon him, he inherited the promise of God to return to the land

which God said that all of the families of the earth would be

blessed through him. God also promised that He would be with

Jacob wherever he was, and in the land He promised to give him.

And Jacob made a covenant with God to return to that place and

to give Him a tenth of all that God would give him.

Jacob, remembered the promise of God and decided he would

trust God to restore him to his brother, and journeyed back to the

land God promised, to reunite with Esau his brother. While on his

journey, Jacob had an encounter with God that changed him

completely. As he approached Esau, Jacob humbled himself before

Esau, and Esau embraced him. Their relationship had been

restored.

(ISV) Gen 33:3 Then he went out to meet Esau, passing in front of all of them, and bowed low to the ground seven times as he approached his brother.

Gen 33:4 Esau ran to meet Jacob and embraced him. Then he fell on his neck and kissed him. And they wept.

We see in this story that trust in God, with humility and honor towards his brother were the determining factors that made the difference. Humility is the foundation to restoration of any relationship. When we teach our children that humility will open the doors of forgiveness, when there seems to be no hope of restoration, they will themselves learn the process of reconciliation as a way of life.

❧We are forgiven so we forgive❧

(ISV) Col 3:12 Therefore, as God's chosen ones, holy and loved, clothe yourselves with compassion, kindness, humility, meekness, and patience.

Col 3:13 Be tolerant of one another and forgive each other if anyone has a complaint against another. Just as the Lord has forgiven you, you also should forgive.

❧I need you to need me❧

God shows us in His word that we are to tolerate one another.

Challenges will arise within the family relationships, but we must

remember that we are a family. There is no individualism in

family, and no one persons need, can be met by their own means.

It requires the aid of another, because that's just the way God

created us. Our attitude should always be, I need you to need me.

Chapter III

Extended Family/Friends & Associate Relationships

There is an age old adage that says "it takes a village to raise a child", yet I would add to that, "it takes a family to become a village".

The family begins with two people, a husband and wife. They bare children, who bare grandchildren, and so on. Until that which began with a nucleus, branches off and with time and distance become a series of nucleuses, that ultimately become extended family, then friends, and finally to associates, a village does not exist. But all in all, going back to the root, which is the original nucleus. We are all family removed multiple times. As with everything else, the bible gives reference to these relationships, that we might build our relationships on the foundations of its word.

By one man and one woman is family given, and God intended us to be one family

Gen 2:24 Therefore shall a man leave his father and his mother, and shall cleave unto his wife: and they shall be one flesh.

Gen 3:20 And Adam called his wife's name Eve; because she was the mother of all living.

It all began with one man and one woman, yet over time with sin entering the world, dissension and destruction began to rule. People began to become lovers of themselves and what God created to be one family, became a mass perversion of family. Relationships began to develop outside of what God originally intended, because of mans own self desire and lust. As we saw in the sibling relationships, people rebelled against each other and the way of the Lord their God. So again, what began with parents trickled down into other relationships, even to extended family, friends and associates. The pattern continued to the children and beyond.

Only through God can the family be restored

The pattern and effects of selfishness, like a dreaded disease spreads from generation to generation, with no end in sight. But, God for saw this and prepared a way to redeem his creation of man along with His intended purpose. The unfortunate thing is that not all men would receive this redemption to gain access to hope and a future. Only through God can the family be restored, by redemption in Christ Jesus.

You must understand that all successful relationships are byproducts of humility and honor. How we chose to interact with others will be the determining factor to the relationship status. The value we place on the life of another will either increase or decrease our own value and self worth. You see even if we have a legitimate quarrel with someone who may be an extended family member, a friend or associate. The process of reconciliation is the same. It starts with forgiveness, which is a byproduct of humility.

Col 3:13 Forbearing one another, and forgiving one another, if any man have a quarrel against any: even as Christ forgave you, so also *do* ye

I cannot stress the importance of the parent, as all things in

regards to relationships, revert back to the parents. God has

instructed parents on how a child becomes a note worthy and

honorable adult.

Deu 11:19 And ye shall teach them your children, speaking of them when thou sittest in thine house, and when thou walkest by the way, when thou liest down, and when thou risest up.
Deu 11:20 And thou shalt write them upon the door posts of thine house, and upon thy gates:
Deu 11:21 That your days may be multiplied, and the days of your children,

We are to express love towards each other, because love is of

God, and those who confess to love God must indeed love their

brother, relative, and friend. It is impossible for man to love,

unless he first has the love of God within him. The same love begins with the redemption of the soul of man which was

poisoned by sin. This redemption allows the love of God to once

again fill the heart of man, enabling him to love others.

❦For love bares all things❧

(ISV) Rom 12:10 Be devoted to each other with mutual affection. Excel at showing respect for each other.
(ISV) Rom 12:11 Never be lazy in showing such devotion. Be on fire with the Spirit. Serve the Lord.
(ISV) Rom 12:12 Be joyful in hope, patient in trouble, and persistent in prayer.
(ISV) Rom 12:13 Supply the needs of the saints. Extend hospitality to strangers.
(ISV) Rom 12:14 Bless those who persecute you. Keep on blessing them, and never curse them.
(ISV) Rom 12:15 Rejoice with those who are rejoicing. Cry with those who are crying.
(ISV) Rom 12:16 Live in harmony with each other. Do not be arrogant, but associate with humble people. Do not think that you are wiser than you really are.

This is what God says love is and how it is to be represented. For love bares all things.

(ISV) 1Co 13:4 Love is always patient; love is always kind; love is never envious or arrogant with pride. Nor is she concerned,

(ISV) 1Co 13:5 and she is never rude; she never thinks just of herself or ever gets annoyed. She never is resentful;

(ISV) 1Co 13:6 is never glad with sin; she's always glad to side with truth, and pleased that truth will win.

1Co 13:7 Beareth all things, believeth all things, hopeth all things, endureth all things.

If anyone fails to provide for or give care to his own, which would encompass his family, his friends, his associates, and yes even his enemy is some cases according to God's standards, is denying the faith. Yes I know it sounds counterproductive to set someone else's interest ahead of your own. But that is the way of God, and the only means of obtaining good success in life, especially with relationships, to which without them there is no life to be lived.

1Ti 5:8 But if any provide not for his own, and specially for those of his own house, he hath denied the faith, and is worse than an infidel.

We have a need to dwell in unity with each other. It is in unity that we are strengthened to deal safely in all of life's challenges. To remain in unity we must be able to exercise forgiveness when issues arise, because they will always certainly come. How we chose to manage the issues when they arise, will set the stage regarding our relationships with extended family, friends, and associates.

Gen 50:17 So shall ye say unto Joseph, Forgive, I pray thee now, the trespass of thy brethren, and their sin; for they did unto thee evil: and now, we pray thee, forgive the trespass of the servants of the God of thy father. And Joseph wept when they spake unto him.

(ISV) **Psa 133:1** Behold, how good and how pleasant *it is* for brethren to dwell together in unity!

We should consider ourselves, how we desire to be treated, or how we would want to be loved. We should never hold grudges toward another person. If we do, that is a clear indication that we probably have a deeper issue that needs to be addressed.

(ISV) Lev 19:18 "You are not to seek vengeance or hold a grudge against the descendants of your people. Instead, love your neighbor as yourself. I am the LORD."

God goes on to say that we should not be indebted to anyone because of anything. Only, that we would owe the debt of loving everyone.

(ISV) Rom 13:8 Do not owe anyone anything—except to love one another. For the one who loves another has fulfilled the Law.

It is critical that our attitude and mindset be one that is in pursuit of living peacefully with everyone. No matter what issues may arise, peace should always be the resolve. This too requires that the overall need of others must be a priority. The power that one person has within them, could build up a great nation, but it can also destroy a great nation with little effort.

(ISV) Rom 14:19 Therefore, let's keep on pursuing those things that bring peace and that lead to building up one another.

☙Good fellowship is a motivator❧

In addition to the pursuit of peace, we are to build up and

encourage each other, while showing appreciation for what the

other party brings to a relationship. Good fellowship is a motivator

towards each person doing good deeds unto another.

(ISV) 1Th 5:11 So then, encourage one another and build each
    other up, as you are doing.
(ISV) 1Th 5:12 Brothers, we ask you to show your appreciation for
those who work among you,
(ISV) Heb 10:24 And let us continue to consider how to motivate
    one another to love and good deeds,
(ISV) Heb 10:25 not neglecting to meet together, as is the habit of
    some, but encouraging one another even more as you see the
    day of the Lord coming nearer.

Chapter IV

Authority/Subordinate Relationships

All human relations must encompass some form of authority and subordinate socialistic standard in the sphere of life in the earth. It is impossible to speak on this subject without considering the origin of authority. Many theologians and the like would stand divided when considering the structure of authority within the scope of deity. So I will take the liberty of setting the record straight, as it has been divinely revealed to me. The order of the authority and subordinate relations within the order of heaven is truly a template for the standard within the earth. The deity itself is the complete authority of all creation. The Father, Son and Holy Spirit make up what is known to many as the trinity or tri-union embodiment of God, they are one. They stand parallel having separate titles and duties as it relates to position yet the same authority equally. The subordinate positions of heaven are assigned to the angelic host and flow downward in tiers representing descending levels of authority under God.The authority within the earth begins with man who has been given authority over all the creation of the earth, reflecting the authority of God over all creation. Now the chain of authority within the human spectrum is more relative to the structure of authority within the angelic host. There are tiers of authority which is how we now come to the authority and subordinate relations.

An *authority* by simple definition is: a group or person with power; a government; an expert.

A *subordinate* is established as; one who is inferior to; or reduced in authority, one who assist; a citizen.

&❧People need people❧&

Like the angelic host, all humankind are, in some form both an authority and subordinate throughout their lifetime. Again as with all forms of relations, authority to subordinate relations begin with parenting and branch off into other forms of authority and subordinate relations. The same representation and care is relevant in order for the systems to be an effective form of socialism. I must emphasize again, that people need people. There would be no societal structure otherwise. There would be no order, but complete chaos.

As we look at our world today, there is much evidence that unless we focus our thoughts and energy on moral correction. Society as we know it, is certainly headed towards that chaos, to where order within the human spectrum will cease to exist. This statement may appear to be extreme, and it is intended to be so, that the seriousness to our demise is recognized. And that it ultimately be dealt with before it's too late.

Why would I make such a statement? Well because our society has succumb to an attitude of every man is right within himself, and this mindset is destroying the structure of hierarchy.

It seems that no one really has respect for authority anymore, and those in authority have diminished their respect and honor for the subordinate or citizen. Consider our world governments, which are the highest level of authority in the earth. They exploit their authority over the people who voted them in, rather than giving way to the desires of the people. The authorities of the world have become an insubordinate society to the authority of God. What does God say about authority and subordinate relationships in His word.

All authority has been established by God

Romans 13;1 says it best, that all people are to be subordinate to the authorities of God, and whoever fails to do so. Subject themselves to the judgment of that authority.

(ASV) Rom 13:1 Let every soul be in subjection to the higher powers: for there is no power but of God; and the *powers* that be are ordained of God.
(ASV) **Rom 13:2** Therefore he that resisteth the power, withstandeth the ordinance of God: and they that withstand shall receive to themselves judgment.

Likewise God has set various authorities in place. I believe that parenting is the highest form of those authorities, because it sets the stage to what the subsequent authorities in the world will be and how they will be administered. The purpose of authority is to establish good works in the earth. As an authority figure, are you prone to establishing good works? Do you set a president to bring out the very best in those who are subordinates under you. Or are you an authority figure who usurps authority for your own self profit. While forcing, your ill will, upon others to advocate your own agenda. Consider that in doing so you are ignoring the principle and instructions of the higher authority. This is considered to be treason and carries a very high level of judgment because your authority affects many, so great will be your judgment. However, if you are one, who adheres to the established authority of God with the purpose to establish good works. To you a reward shall be given, because even though you sit in a place of authority. You have subjected yourself as a subordinate under the authority of God.

❧When we are submitted to His authority the kingdom prospers❧

As a subordinate under authority, understand that the authority is only as effective as those who represent and support it. For example, we are considered to be and are ambassadors unto God within His earthly kingdom. When we are submitted to His authority the kingdom prospers. But, if we exploit and usurp our own authority, the kingdom fails because there is no power in the authority we have. Accept we be under God's authority, only then do we have access to the power required to prosper the kingdom. The ultimate authority is in God's power.

To be constant to the protocol established by God, it is necessary that we be subject to the authorities over us. They are ministers to the order of God's creation, and their time and efforts are devoted to God and to us. We are to also be obligated to pay our

just due in taxes and in honor to those authorities.

(ISV) Rom 13:5 Therefore, it is necessary for you to be acquiescent
   to the authorities, not only for the sake of God's punishment,
   but also for the sake of your own conscience.
(ISV) Rom 13:6 This is also why you pay taxes. For rulers are
   God's servants faithfully devoting themselves to their work.

The importance of the true value in this particular relationship is

the cornerstone to every relationship that does exist between God

and man, and one man to another man. We cannot afford to

continue in ignorance in regards to the devastation that occurs

every single day that we stand by and do nothing, towards

securing our future. The hierarchy of societal order is splitting at

the seams, because people at large have taken authority into their

own hands. And have created a hierarchy within themselves. Have

you ever watched a barrel of crabs? You will never see a single

crab reach the top of the barrel. That is because, every one of them have the same goal which is to reach the top of the barrel to freedom. Even at the expense of pulling down and destroying one of their own. This is what our world has come to, and ultimately all of the crabs in the barrel die, because the habitat and order to which they live and thrive, has been reduced to a barrel with no life sustaining order to it. Selfishness personified.

❧A man alone will die alone, at his own hand❧

Selfishness is the primary attribute of one who is lazy. Not wanting to serve anyone or anything, except themselves. In all actuality, they don't even care for themselves, because the principle and protocol of God in the earth's kingdom, is for every man to serve the other. A man alone will die alone, at his own hand.

(ISV) Pro 6:9 How long will you lie down, lazy man? When will you get up from your sleep?
(ISV) Pro 6:10 A little sleep, a little slumber, a little folding of the

hands to rest,
(ISV) Pro 6:11 and your poverty will come on you like a bandit and your desperation like an armed man.
(ISV) Pro 6:12 A worthless man, a wicked man, goes around with devious speech,
(ISV) Pro 6:13 winking with his eyes, making signs with his feet, pointing with his fingers,
(ISV) Pro 6:14 planning evil with a perverse mind, continually stirring up discord.
(ISV) Pro 6:15 Therefore, disaster will overtake him suddenly. He will be broken in an instant, and he will never recover

I conclude by asking this question. Would you be like the ant, who

subject themselves to one another that together they may gather

what is necessary for survival. Or shall you chose to be like the

crab in a barrel who claws it's way to the top, only to find that

they have never left the bottom of the barrel.

True value is in how one serves, for without serving how can a value be given

Chapter V

Teacher/Student Relationships

The teacher and student relationship is one of the most import

and most powerful relationships within the human spectrum of

life. The teacher is in a position of authority which requires one to

have the ability to lead, guide, instruct, influence, and in some

cases even control those who are subject to their instruction or

coaching. The teacher must also have the ability to be sensitive to

the needs, personality, desire, potential, talent, and gifts, of the

student who is under their influence. This person who is the

teacher must be a discerner of the character of the student and

possess the wisdom to direct or redirect the mindset of that

individual in a private and personal setting, or individuals within a

classroom setting. The

student on the other hand should understand that he or she has the responsibility to respect and obey the authority of the teacher. There is customarily a mutual understanding and a common practice in society at large. However in light of how societal practices have turned the corner from being a unified common ground for people in society to balance and manage social development with the intended purpose of mankind living in peace, and not being subject to chaos. We now are on a rapid pace to establishing chaos in a society that has almost completely abandoned the concept of the teacher being in a place of authority over the student. This practice has even ventured over, into the private lives of parents raising their children within the walls of their own homes. This is a major and rapidly growing destructive process that must be corrected if we are to continue a society of order, with respect for all.

&Everybody being free to live as they please is a fallacy&

The principles from which all modern societal infrastructures have been developed and maintained over centuries, from the time man inhabited the earth until now, have been diminished even disposed of in some cases. The idea of everybody being free to live as they please is a fallacy. Especially when you consider that those who chose to maintain the principles which have been originally established by the creator of the earth and man, are continuously along with those principles expunged from being considered as a valid proponent to today's society.

This behavior of radical insubordination to the creator has undoubtedly subjected mankind and the earth to the judgment of God, in this life and throughout eternity. What can you do to soften the blow of God's judgment to your home and your society?

Let's look at and consider what God has to say regarding the

relationship of teacher and student.

I would ascribe the future of our society to the book of Romans

chapter 15, vs. 4 as the ideal starting point to the restoring of

what has been lost in society today, as it relates to any hope that

we might have, to a good future for generations to come.

(ASV) Rom 15:4 For whatsoever things were written aforetime
were written for our learning, that through patience and
through comfort of the scriptures we might have hope.

➰ We will see the evidence of God's presence and power ➰

We see here that it is imperative that we be comforted, through exercising patience, in knowing that the word God has given us to live by, stands true and mighty. Especially in troubled times when it seems that perhaps God is not even present anymore. If we stand on His truth, in the midst of society at large shaking its fist at us, and the principles of God by which we live. We will see the evidence of God's presence and power overcome, for there are yet many who will join us in our righteous stand for God and His kingdom here in the earth.

❧By faith God's purpose must stand☙

It is quite clear that teaching is not for everyone. If someone who is not qualified to teach, does indeed teach. This then would be the cause as to how the world society has spun into a cycle which has become a vacuum to the destruction of the order of society. Those who are full of wisdom are responsible to speak out against those who have been given a voice of deception to deceive the people through manipulation. By faith it's God's purpose that must stand.

(ISV) 1Ti 1:3 When I was on my way to Macedonia, I urged you to stay in Ephesus so that you could instruct certain people to stop teaching false doctrine

(ISV) 1Ti 1:4 and occupying themselves with myths and endless genealogies. These things promote controversies rather than God's ongoing purpose, which involves faith.

We are warned of what will become of society if we fail to heed God's instruction and commandments. Without people who have a heart to discern the times, and the doctrines of truth that our younger generations are taught. They would have absolutely no hope of a future here in the earth, and especially not with God. Those who are qualified and those who are filled with wisdom must cry out with a loud voice to overcome the chatter of those who have been given a voice of deception. What they say seems right but it is far from the truth, and the truth must be told or many will die from their belief in a lie, having never heard the truth. Who will be held accountable to those who have been lost, it's the teacher. So always be ready to give a true account to those who will hear you, and those who chose not to listen are responsible to themselves and God.

(ISV) 2Ti 4:2 to proclaim the message. Be ready to do this whether or not the time is convenient. Refute, warn, and encourage with the utmost patience when you teach.

(ISV) 2Ti 4:3 For the time will come when people will not tolerate healthy doctrine, but with itching ears will surround themselves with teachers who cater to their people's own desires.

(ISV) 2Ti 4:4 They will refuse to listen to the truth and will turn to myths.

In our homes, in our churches, in our facilities of higher education, it is said that the student is not greater than the teacher. However I say that we must always carry the attitude that the student is greater, for they are our future now, and if we fail to set a precedent that the future of the generations to come are more important than our present. We would have failed the commission from God to teach them. By seeing them greater and their future more important, epitomizes the power of self through selfless acts of mercy, grace, kindness, and love.

(ISV) Php 2:1 Therefore, if there is any encouragement in the Messiah, if there is any comfort of love, if there is any fellowship in the Spirit, if there is any compassion and sympathy,

(ISV) **Php 2:2** then fill me with joy by having the same attitude, sharing the same love, being united in spirit, and keeping one purpose in mind.

(ISV) Php 2:3 Do not act out of selfish ambition or conceit, but with humility think of others as being better than yourselves.

The awesome responsibility of teaching the truth is for every Christian that the truth be heard and known by their actions, in the home, on the job, in the schools, at social events etc.. Wherever people can be found, the opportunity for them to know and for you to teach what is right and true is commanded by God. Those who are called to teach have a greater responsibility to always in every occasion give way to the opportunity to share the wisdom and knowledge that God has given them. There is also a greater penalty for those who fail to teach, wasting the gift given by God. Let us who are responsible parties to our future generations, who teach, not neglect our partnership with Him,

that the power of self within you, would fulfill its God given

purpose.

(ISV) Heb 3:14 because we are the Messiah's partners only if we
   hold on to our original confidence to the end.
(ISV) Heb 10:25 not neglecting to meet together, as is the habit of
   some, but encouraging one another even more as you see the
   day of the Lord coming nearer.

Chapter VI

Employer/Employee Relationships

The employer and employee relationship could be considered one of the most interesting and challenging of all of the relationships represented in this book. In this reference, you will notice that it appears that the employee might be at a disadvantage as it relates to what is expected of them. It would also appear that the employer has the upper hand, because of the authority and power that comes with being the employer. The truth of the matter is that the employee really stands in the position that is most essential to the employer and employee relationship. The business of the employer could not possibly survive or even exist without what the employee brings to the business. This type of relationship, more than any thus far, I believe truly represents the concept of "The Power of Self". In this book, the representation that people need people and the idea that God created and purposed in us, to have within us everything that the other person needs to survive and even excel or increase in life. When a person is able to grasp this idea and begin to live by it. It then becomes inevitable that the value of that person will literally increase, and their worth becomes a desirable commodity to many. The word of God has much to say about this type of relationship, to the employer and the employee. But more is directed to the employee than it is to the employer.

❧The employee really stands in the position that is most essential☙

As an employee, you are responsible to be sincere in all you do, where it concerns your employment. You are given guidelines and instructions by your employer that you must adhere to, thus being an obedient worker. Always give your very best effort in your work, especially when your employer is not looking to see what you are doing. God is always watching and expects, to see you at

your best.

(ISV) Col 3:22 Slaves, obey your earthly masters in everything, not
only while being watched in order to please them, but with a
sincere heart, fearing the Lord.

(ISV) Col 3:23 Whatever you do, work at it wholeheartedly as
though you were doing it for the Lord and not merely for
people.

(ISV) Col 3:24 You know that it is from the Lord that you will
receive the inheritance as a reward. It is the Lord Messiah whom
you are serving!

There should never be any display of bias or favoritism

The obligation and attitude of an employer, should be one of

respect towards their employee, with fairness in how the

employee is treated in the company of others and privately. The

employer's position is simple, and that is primarily that the

employee should be given the very best environment and

opportunity to fulfill their employment obligations with honor.

As an employer there should never be any display of bias or favoritism from one employee to the next, regardless of the relationship an employee might have with the employer outside of employment.

Col 4:1 Masters, give unto *your* servants that which is just and equal; knowing that ye also have a Master in heaven.

✦Obedience will reflect your loyalty and commitment✦

Again, a greater emphasis is placed upon the employee to serve the employer, always maintaining a level of obedience that will reflect your loyalty and commitment to your work and employer, and also your relationship with Christ. A higher standard is placed on the employee, because he holds a higher value to the relationship. The servant is always the most important element is a situation to where their effort is required to support the efforts of another.

Eph 6:5 Servants, be obedient to them that are *your* masters according to the flesh, with fear and trembling, in singleness of your heart, as unto Christ;

❧The employer will always look first to the one whom they can trust❧

It is imperative that an employer is able to trust the one who is in their employee. The employer is completely exposed, as they must give the employee access to information and resources to which they depend upon to make their business a successful one. This type of exposure in the hands of someone who is untrustworthy could bring disaster to the business of the employer. As an employee you are obligated to treat everything the employer gives you access to with the same care that you would your very own. The display or evidence of trustworthiness will in most cases, cause an employer to give a high level of consideration to you the employee, when task that require special care arise. Yes the

employer will always look first to the one whom they can trust.

Understand that your conduct and trustworthiness may open

doors for you to share with your employer and co-workers the

source of your attitude, which would then cause them to be

attracted to God.

Pro 25:13 **As the cold of snow in the time of harvest,** *so is* **a faithful messenger to them that send** him: for he refresheth the soul of his masters.
(ISV) Tit 2:9 Slaves are to submit to their masters in everything, aiming to please them and not argue with them
(ISV) Tit 2:10 or steal from them. Instead, they are to show complete and perfect loyalty, so that in every way they may make the teaching about God our Savior more attractive.

❧Diligence will expand your sphere of influence☙

As an employee, consider that it is to your advantage and benefit

to be diligent at your job. Even in the midst of harsh and unfair

treatment from an employer. Always be willing to do more than what is expected of you. Of course not to the point of suffering

abuse, but knowing that God is with you, and your reward is with

Him, because of your representation of righteousness.

When your attitude is to glorify God as you are challenged on your

job, He will protect you and always prepare an exit strategy for

you, and you will increase because you allowed God to do it for

you, instead of having your own way.

There are many advantages to being diligent in your work and

place of employment. Case and point, diligence will;

- ➢ Please God

- ➢ Earn you recognition and respect with your employer and
  co-workers

- ➢ Improve your reputation and character

- ➢ Increase you in knowledge and experience

➢ Develop your spiritual maturity

➢ Expand your sphere of influence

(ISV) Gen 31:42 If the God of my father—the God of Abraham, the God whom Isaac feared—had not been with me, you would have sent me away empty handed. But God saw my misery and how hard I've worked with my own hands—and he rebuked you last night."

In today's society it is common to hear of people making grave complaints against their employer, or threatening strike, and even filing lawsuits against them. But God speaks very adamantly and clearly about how these situations are to be dealt with. He begins by instructing that we be content in what we have, as it relates to the wages we have accepted for our employee.

(ISV) Luk 3:14 Even some soldiers were asking him, "And what should we do?" He told them, "Never extort money from anyone by threats or blackmail, and be satisfied with your pay."

✒Practice being content✒

God said He would never leave you or abandon you. Again, I say practice being content, knowing that God is your source. Do not become bound by money and it's power to influence your lifestyle. You will find yourself chasing money and not living your life. Money is only to be a tool to enable you to acquire resources.

(ISV) Heb 13:5 Keep your lives free from the love of money, and be content with what you have, for God has said, "I will never leave you or abandon you."

Some employers may be very strict and even unrealistic in their concept of how an employee is expected to perform on the job. But even so, you as the employee should always submit and respect the employers company and job that you signed on to do. Your integrity to what you committed to when you accepted the job offer is what you should hold fast to, until a better opportunity comes available to you.

(ISV) 1Pe 2:18 You household servants must submit yourselves to your masters out of respect, not only to those who are kind and fair, but also to those who are unjust.

❧Ambition, will always make room for you to advance in life☙

Set in your daily thoughts, that in all that you do you are doing it as though, you were doing it for God directly. This mindset will lead you into ambition as a way of life. Ambition will always make room for you to advance in life and in anything you do in life. See yourself working for the Lord. See Him as your employer, and do not focus on the man that God has provided to employee you.

(ISV) Col 3:23 Whatever you do, work at it wholeheartedly as though you were doing it for the Lord and not merely for people.

It is not profitable for a man to pursue great gain in worldly things

Jesus, in his own words said that it is not profitable for a man to pursue great gain in worldly things or accolades. Never over extend yourself in the employee of another, seeking to be promoted, or gain financial increase. Simply allow your integrity and diligence to make way for you to acquire good success. I say good success, because all success is not good. Having promotion or financial gain as your primary motive for what you do, will make you a slave to money, and fame. Eventually your character will falter, and even your very soul could be at stake. That is not a price anyone should be willing to pay for a temporary and false pleasure.

(ISV) Luk 9:25 What profit will a person have if he gains the whole world, but destroys himself or is lost?

You being an employer or employee, must position yourself to be respected by your employee or employer, that your business or their job does not overshadow your commitment and responsibility to God and yourself and your family. There is just no possible way that you can be fully committed to God and be fully committed to the things of this world. One must take precedence over the other. A decision must be made between God and the world. The decision is easy, choose God.

(ISV) Mat 6:24 "No one can serve two masters, because either he will hate one and love the other, or be loyal to one and despise the other. You cannot serve God and riches!"

❧If Christ did it, so can you❧

We can and should follow Christ's example, to always live for righteousness sake. The overall theme here is to be a servant to all.

There is great power to which one individual holds within himself, to build up the lives of people and shape the world in the process of doing so, by simply placing the desire and need of another above your own desire and need. This is a principle that God has instituted from the creation of man, and it is unique only to man. No other created system is established in this manner. Christ Jesus knew and understood exactly what His purpose for being here in the earth was. He did not ever deviate from what his assignment was. He pressed on until His assignment was completed, in victory. If Christ did it, so can you.

(ISV) 1Pe 2:13 For the Lord's sake submit yourselves to every human authority: whether to the king as supreme,
(ISV) 1Pe 2:14 or to governors who are sent by him to punish those who do wrong and to praise those who do right.
(ISV) 1Pe 2:15 For it is God's will that by doing right you should silence the ignorant talk of foolish people.
(ISV) 1Pe 2:16 Live like free people, and do not use your freedom as an excuse for doing evil. Instead, be God's servants.

(ISV) 1Pe 2:17 Honor everyone. Keep on loving the community of believers, fearing God, and honoring the king.

(ISV) 1Pe 2:18 You household servants must submit yourselves to your masters out of respect, not only to those who are kind and fair, but also to those who are unjust.

(ISV) 1Pe 2:19 For it is a fine thing if, when moved by your conscience to please God, you suffer patiently when wronged.

(ISV) 1Pe 2:20 What good does it do if, when you sin, you patiently receive punishment for it? But if you suffer for doing good and receive it patiently, you have God's approval.

(ISV) 1Pe 2:21 This is, in fact, what you were called to do, because: The Messiah also suffered for you and left an example for you to follow in his steps.

(ISV) 1Pe 2:22 "He never sinned, and he never told a lie."

(ISV) 1Pe 2:23 When he was insulted, he did not retaliate. When he suffered, he did not threaten. It was his habit to commit the matter to the one who judges fairly.

(ISV) 1Pe 2:24 "He himself bore our sins" in his body on the tree, so that we might die to those sins and live righteously. "By his wounds you have been healed."

(ISV) 1Pe 2:25 You were "like sheep that kept going astray," but now you have returned to the shepherd and overseer of your souls.

Chapter VII

Boyfriend/Girlfriend Relationships

An unprotected heart is an end road to disaster

The demise of our future generations hinge largely on the inability

of our young people to effectively choose and develop healthy

friendships, and understand their purpose in boyfriend /girlfriend

relationships. This is largely due to the failure of society to

properly inform them as to what is morally correct and what is

not.

God instructs, and even warns that we are to guard our hearts

above all things. All life begins within the affections of our hearts.

The hearts is fueled by emotion and is not able think, or give

consideration to making decisions on its own accord. Decisions

that involve the heart, require the aid or assistance and influence of the mind and the knowledge and wisdom that drives it. The source of which knowledge and wisdom are acquired, will inevitably lead to a place of decision that ultimately determines the outcome of how people live their lives. An unprotected heart is an end road to disaster.

(ISV) Pro 4:23 Above everything else guard your heart, because from it flow the springs of life.

When considering knowledge, know that it always leads to wisdom. But, because all knowledge is not good, make a habit of evaluating the environment and the people that you choose to associate with. Associating with people, who may not have your best interest in mind, may lead to them having a very powerful and deceptive influence over you. Such an influence could cause you to abandon or discredit the moral standard that may have been instilled in you.

Overcoming such deceptions are in most cases, very difficult and is likely improbable that you will overcome them. Accept, by the effective intervention of the word of God. Along with the assistance of people around you, who live by the word and will hold you accountable.

(ISV) 1Co 15:33 Stop being deceived: "Wicked friends lead to evil ends."

The idea of exercising diligence in the choosing of who you will associate with is very important to your future and present life style. This holds true whether it's a basic friendship among your peers or an intimate relationship between a boy and girl. This particular reference is pertaining specifically to youth and young adults. However it would also be relevant to unmarried adults, which is an aspect that we will look at later.

As much as you are able, be diligent in the choosing of your friends and the potential mate that would be considered for the development of relationships with you. They should have similarities to you, where it concerns how they live and what they believe. In being more specific, this relates to religious and spiritual ideals that generally shapes the moral convictions of the heart. They should love God like you love God.

> (ISV) 2Co 6:14 Stop becoming unevenly yoked with unbelievers. What partnership can righteousness have with lawlessness? What fellowship can light have with darkness?

❧You must avoid peer pressures influence on your decisions☙

Intimate relationships between youth take on a different format in comparison to the relationships between young adults, and adults. There is a vast difference in the purpose of the relationships. For example, the focus of a relationship among youth, should be that you are simply friends, seeking to share in the enjoyment of each others company, and to have fun together. In your relationship experience, you will also aid each other in the development of your personalities by your interactions with each other. As you approach becoming young adults, you will at some point begin to consider your future relationships in a similar manner as you would your career goals. You will experience many changes in your desires and perceptions, while developing your personality and character.

You should avoid allowing peer pressure to influence your decisions. It is never wise to just give into doing what seems to be the popular thing, because everybody is doing it. The bible is filled with wisdom, to guide you in your decision making. As I suggested in the beginning, guard your heart.

Now with young adults and adults, the scope of the relationships purpose is broader. These relationships will more likely be two people headed towards potentially spending their lives together as mates. There is much to give consideration to when taking such a major step in life.

The most important factor is love. But you must ask yourself, is it really love that's being experienced and considered? Some very key points to referencing this consideration of love are;

> Do you exercise **patience** with each other?

> Do you show **kindness** towards each other?

> Do you avoid being **envious** of each other?

> Is **humility** in the character of your relationship?

> Do you avoid being **rude** to each other?

➢ Do you show evidence of being **selfless**?

➢ Do you keep yourselves from **anger** towards each other?

➢ Do you avoid keeping tabs of who is **wrong**?

➢ Is **truth** the foundation of your relationship, nothing

hidden?

➢ Do you **protect** each other from intrusions?

➢ Do you maintain **trust** as the cornerstone of your

relationship?

(ISV) 1Co 13:4 Love is always patient; love is always kind; love is
never envious or arrogant with pride. Nor is she conceited,
(ISV) 1Co 13:5 and she is never rude; she never thinks just of
herself or ever gets annoyed. She never is resentful;
(ISV) 1Co 13:6 is never glad with sin; she's always glad to side with
truth, and pleased that truth will win.
(ISV) 1Co 13:7 She bears up under everything; believes the best in
all; there is no limit to her hope, and never will she fall.

The answers to the questions presented in the previous section will determine your next step. The reference to these questions can be reviewed in I Corinthians 13th chapter. If you answered yes, then you are truly on the path to a great relationship, and I would suggest that it be reinforced with wise counsel. If on the other hand you answered no to any of those questions, then there is still much work to do, which should begin with the two of you having an in depth discussions about any possible future together, and the issues you might be facing. Again I suggest that it be reinforced with wise counsel by a third party who is not bias, and trained to guide you in all wisdom.

This next topic is relative to and directed towards all of the groups represented as unmarried. Your sexual purity is the most treasured possession you have, as it relates to your true value and "The power of Self". This is the one thing that God created in you that is to be reserved for only that special person to whom you would spend your life serving. And that is your spouse. There is a very specific reason why we are admonished to refrain from having sexual relations outside of marriage. The reason is that when two people, a man and a woman engage in intercourse, your spirit and soul merge together. Merge defined in Webster's dictionary is; to unite or bring together as one. Other words that are synonymous with merge are; unify, fuse, combine, unite, blend, commingle. As you can see, these are very powerful and very permanent terminologies. The indication here is that two become as one, just as God said in His word.

So when you have commingled yourself with others, who were not your soul mate whom is intended especially for you. You become contaminated, corrupted, or defiled, and polluted. Yes, those are strong words, because my goal is to get you to realize how important this is as it relates to the purpose of your being as God intended, and the effect it would have in your purpose being fulfilled. If the earth is filled with contamination, then it cannot thrive as God intended in His unique and personal design. The responsibility has been place on us to flee the temptation of this defilement.

❧Bad company will corrupt your character❧

I, remind you that bad company will corrupt your character. If you Act, on the following temptations of fulfilling desires of lust that are imposed upon you by people who have already been defiled. It is very dangerous, and selfish on your part. You have neglected to consider your mate. And so you risk not ever finding that person. If by chance you do find that person, your relationship in all likelihood would never reach the level of intimacy that was intended by God.

Only through the merciful act of God imparting His grace to your relationship, will you then find some level of solace in your relationship. But it will still fall short of its original value and purpose.

It takes an act of being selfless, when conforming to the pursuit of God's original plan for your purposeful life with the mate He has for you. I will share in the next chapter, the many benefits of being selfless, and to waiting on God and your mate.

(ISV) 1Co 6:18 Keep on running away from sexual immorality. Any other sin that a person commits is outside his body, but the person who sins sexually sins against his own body.

What are your intentions, when you find yourself attracted to someone of the opposite sex? Are you drawn to them in a way that causes your desire to burn with passion? Do you find yourself lingering and giving way to imagining what it might be like to be with them? This is the time that you should flee, because you have fallen to sin, and much danger is ahead of you.

As you flee, have a change of heart. Repent, by confessing your sin to God. He will allow you a new and fresh start. He cares for you and will help you overcome these feelings, if you ask Him, and allow Him to. Give yourself to God, in pursuit of the selfless act of waiting for your mate. In that you will discover your true value.

(ISV) Mat 5:28 But I say to you, anyone who stares at a woman with lust for her has already committed adultery with her in his heart.

Chapter VIII

Husband/Wife Relationships

❧The husband/wife unit was designed to reflect the image, likeness, and unity of the godhead❧

Without the relationship of a husband and wife, which is one man and one women. There would be no family and most certainly the human race would not exist. The husband and wife unit was created and designed to reflect the image and likeness of the unity that is in the godhead. That is one unit which is in total and perfect harmony. It is also purposed to mirror God's relationship with His creation, the human race.

The love that God the father extends to His children has no special conditions attached to it, and is full of grace. His love is patient, His love is kind, His love does not envy, His love does not boast,

His love is not arrogant, His love is not rude, His love does not insist on having its own way, (however, we must choose Him and receive His love), His love is not irritable, His love is not resentful. This is the same love that we are to express towards our spouse. This is perfect love and it will cast out all of the many types of fear and deception, which would attempt to launch an attack against marriage.

This final chapter shall take us back to the very beginning of the creation of man. In this chapter you will discover the true value of a man and the true value of a woman. Although they differ vastly, they are in very close proximity as it relates to value and purpose. The primary differences are in their functionality leading to the fulfillment of purpose.

God desired that within the earth He created, there would be a representation of Himself, having the same likeness of what is represented in heaven, as in the godhead. So he created man, in His image and likeness. He gave them dominion over their kingdom He called the earth. Man was and is to rule on earth as God does, in heaven. He then blessed them and instructed them to multiply and replenish the earth. God provided everything that was required to enable them to fulfill their created purpose.

Now you might say that the image and likeness of God is a tri-part being and man is only a two-part being. Well the truth is that when God, breath His breath into the body, soul, and spirit of man. His Spirit at that very moment became a part of the man He created, making man a tri-part being, just like God. This is when all the generations of the earth were created.

The man and woman began as one spirit, with a dual functionality being male and female within itself. After God formed the man from the earth, and gave him life. God decided that the male and female should be separated, becoming man and women for the purpose of individual functionality and fellowship in the earth. Until then, mans only fellowship aside from God was with the animals and the earth (nature). God saw that after the separation of the male and female spirit being and then rejoining them each in their own body, the fellowship in the natural was good. And it pleased Him greatly.

Gen 1:27 So God created man in his *own* image, in the image of God created he him; male and female created he them.

Eph 5:28 So ought men to love their wives as their own bodies. He that loveth his wife loveth himself.

Endless acts of selflessness are what will enable two people to become as one

This perfect love, which is the foundation, even the cornerstone of the marriage relationship. Is the spark that ignites "The Power of Self" within the individuals and the relationship alike. Endless acts of selflessness are what will enable two people to become as one, as each person provides the fulfillment that the other person is lacking. This is a matter of principle, and from the beginning, as God's word reveals to us, it is an indestructible part of God's creation. When principles, are ignored or misrepresented it will only lead to chaos and destruction. When the family structure is out of order, it spreads from generation to generation, causing society and the world to suffer. The order as God has established it to be, is that a man should detach himself from his parents home and rule, in order to attach himself to his wife and establish his own home and rule. According to the principles of God, this is the proper order of family business. And so when a man takes a wife to himself, he should even consider himself and how much he loves his own body. This is the same consideration he shall give to his wife, who is now a part of him. In this you treat your wife as you would yourself, and even above yourself, by that, through her you fulfill your own self need and purpose. What you desire and require is in her, and the only possible way of extracting from her what you need, is to selflessly give her what she needs from you. Your selflessness becomes your wholeness, and that is your true value

Eph 5:31 For this cause shall a man leave his father and mother, and shall be joined unto his wife, and they two shall be one flesh.

Eph 5:32 This is a great mystery: but I speak concerning Christ and the church.

Eph 5:33 Nevertheless let every one of you in particular so love his wife even as himself; and the wife *see* that she reverence *her* husband.

Eph 5:25 Husbands, love your wives, even as Christ also loved the church, and gave himself for it;

As a wife you are to submit yourself to your husband's love, leadership and authority. In it, he will care for you even as Christ does His own body. He will provide for you, protect you, edify you, encourage you, cherish you, uphold you, and reveal to you and expose you to the love of Christ. This submission does not put you in a place of subordination. You are his equal to walk along side him as a co-laborer and a helper in fulfilling your God given purpose, just the same as Christ is equal with God and co-laborer with Him in fulfilling the Kingdom and His promises to His bride, the church.

Eph 5:22 Wives, submit yourselves unto your own husbands, as unto the Lord.

Eph 5:23 For the husband is the head of the wife, even as Christ is the head of the church: and he is the saviour of the body.

Eph 5:24 Therefore as the church is subject unto Christ, so *let* the wives *be* to their own husbands in everything.

❧The bible is the most explicit, provocative, sensual, and complete book on sexual relations❧

The bible is the most explicit, the most provocative, the most sensual and the most complete book on sexual relations between a man and a women ever written. Consider that if people would use it as the final authority that it is. Oh, what a different world view we would have on the institution of marriage. The picture we would see would not be a 51% divorce rate in the Christian community, which would undoubtedly affect the world perspective on marriage and family. Men would honor women rather than exploit and abused them as if they are an object of ownership. But even so, the bible speaks of being a good steward over that which is owned. Women would have a respect for men that honors them as the leaders that they are responsible for being.

Women would also willingly and effortlessly submit to the authority of the men whom they are espoused to.

The marriage bed is to be a sacred place and undefiled. The thoughts and images of the world should have no place in the home, and especially not in the bedroom. This is primarily directed to husbands, because men have a tendency to carry their past experiences into their marriage.

This is an age old problem that the bible speaks to very specifically, in saying that even if a man looks at a woman who is not his wife in a lustful manner, then he has sin by committing adultery. This kind of behavior is also one of the key factors leading to men being fixated on pornography. An issue we take far too lightly, pornography in many cases can be much more addictive and more destructive than any drug addiction. Jesus in his own words has warned against this practice, and even so has given specific instruction as to how we should avoid paying the

severe penalty of such sin.

(ASV)Mat 5:28 but I say unto you, that every one that looketh on a
woman to lust after her hath committed adultery with her
already in his heart.

(ASV)Mat 5:29 And if thy right eye causeth thee to stumble, pluck
it out, and cast it from thee: for it is profitable for thee that one
of thy members should perish, and not thy whole body be cast
into hell.

❧Flee from any form of sexual immorality❧

The bibles reference on this subject is not merely for men alone,

but addresses everyone. Husbands, wives, adult singles, young

adults and adolescents. God clearly said that we must flee from

any form of sexual immorality, because if you don't, you sin

against your own body, and the repercussion from it is truly more

devastating than sins committed outside of the body.

Know and understand that your body is not your own.

It is the temple of God's Holy Spirit first, after having been

redeemed by His grace and then it's also been reserved for the

spouse that you do or will spend your life with.

(ASV)1Co 6:18 Flee fornication. Every sin that a man doeth is
without the body; but he that committeth fornication sinneth
against his own body.
(ASV)1Co 6:19 Or know ye not that your body is a temple of the
Holy Spirit which is in you, which ye have from God? and ye
are not your own;

A message to husbands and wives also. *It is your conduct toward*

your spouse that will determine the quality of life you have

together. Sexual immorality begins as a temptation, and is fueled

by ones lack in receiving what is rightfully theirs, to receive in the

marriage relationship only.

Forgive each other and let love be your garment that covers

In other words, it would not only be selfish, but also an act of dissimulation that would create a barrier of untrustworthiness between you. Before long you would then find communication and understanding is nonexistent. The conduct of being selfless and giving attention to your spouse will ultimately lead to you receiving all that you need and desire from your spouse, without struggle. So I admonish you to not think so much of yourself and what is best for you, but what is best for your spouse. It will protect you from having issues of venturing outside of your marriage, and in the case to where this may have already occurred in the past, it will deliver you from that and move you towards a brighter future together. Most of all, forgive each other and let love be your garment that covers.

(ISV)1Co 7:2 Nevertheless, *to avoid* fornication, let every man have his own wife, and let every woman have her own husband.
(ISV)1Co 7:3 Let the husband render unto the wife due benevolence: and likewise also the wife unto the husband.

(ISV)Php 2:3 Do not act out of selfish ambition or conceit, but with humility think of others as being better than yourselves.
(ISV)Php 2:4 Do not be concerned about your own interests, but also be concerned about the interests of others.

(ISV)Col 3:13 Be tolerant of one another and forgive each other if anyone has a complaint against another. Just as the Lord has forgiven you, you also should forgive.
(ISV)Col 3:14 Above all, clothe yourselves with love, which ties everything together in unity.

❧You are responsible for the destructive effects your actions have on society❧

Learn how to chose your battles, by avoiding unnecessary quarrels that could result in major blow-ups, without a justifiable cause.

Fighting, typically has no merit in a marriage relationship and is almost always due to someone's own selfishness and inadequacies that are generally denied.

The desire to have things your way, or wanting something you see in others will thrust you into destructive behavior, and it's always the marriage and family that suffers. But what is most unfortunate is that the destruction does not end within the walls of marriage and family. It overreaches the confines of the home and spills into society, effecting everyone that becomes involved, and over time even those who aren't the wiser as to what took place in your marriage. Yes you are responsible for the destructive effects your actions have on society at large. In my experience as a relationship counselor, I have found it to be true that, many of the battles that are waged, is a direct result of assumptions within the marriage relationship. Subliminal communications, expected to be taken literally from one party to the other. The mouth is the most powerful and most effective tool of communication in existence.

To ask or to say is the only proper form of communication, which effectively and fully addresses another individual. Even then one must be certain that what the intended communication is to represent, is what the receiving party understands it to be. Again much of the behavior spoken of is learned from the world, instead of the word of God, and has become an acceptable way among Christians. As Christians you are to be the example to the world, not a follower of the world's way. The scripture reference following this paragraph could actually be a definition for selfishness.

(ISV)Jas 4:1 Where do those fights and quarrels among you come from? They come from your selfish desires that are at war in your bodies, don't they?

(ISV)Jas 4:2 You want something but do not get it, so you commit murder. You covet something but cannot obtain it, so you quarrel and fight. You do not get things because you do not ask for them!

(ISV)Jas 4:3 You ask for something but do not get it because you ask for it for the wrong reason—for your own pleasure.

❧A loving heart can overcome anything❧

Resist lustful desires of self gratification by submitting to God's word and His way. When you do this, the suggestions and influences of the devil will leave you alone. As you draw closer to God, and place your trust in Him, you will develop a singleness of mind. In other words your greatest influence will be your knowledge of God's word and your trust in Him will increase, guarding you from the deceptions of the evil one. God wants to come close to you, that He might purify your heart. A pure heart is a loving heart, and *a loving heart can overcome anything*.

(ISV)Jas 4:7 Therefore, submit yourselves to God. Resist the devil, and he will run away from you.

(ISV)Jas 4:8 Come close to God, and he will come close to you. Cleanse your hands, you sinners, and purify your hearts, you double-minded.

So the question I now would have you to consider for yourself is this. What are your intentions toward your spouse? Is it to boast in your own ability and successes? Is it to fulfill your own self indulgences? If you find that your answer registers anywhere remotely close to yes, in these areas. Then I want to admonish you to seek change in your behavior. Because you are entertaining evil, and having known the word, especially even now that you have been made aware of what is right. If you continue in a way that is contrary to what you now know is right, that choice makes you guilty of sin.

(ISV)Jas 4:16 But you boast about your proud intentions. All such boasting is evil.

(ISV)Jas 4:17 Therefore, anyone who knows what is right but fails to do it is guilty of sin.

❧The challenge to do right or wrong is a choice everyone must make❧

Living out this life as a Christian, you are required to live a life that is dead to sin, and the way of the world, while at the same time living a life that is set apart unto the things of God. Being set apart, indicates that you alone according to your own will have chosen a sacrificial lifestyle, which commands you to deny the lust of the flesh and the lust of the eyes. Those are the areas of your existence that causes you to entertain sin. It is the part of you that has not yet been redeemed. If, you have received Christ in your heart and confessed with your mouth, that He is the son of God and has taken your sins, and the penalty for them unto Himself. Then you are truly redeemed and made righteous. But please understand that the reference of your redemption is in part and not fully completed. You are a spirit which has been redeemed. You live in a body of flesh which will be redeemed at the sound of the last trumpet, when Christ returns to receive all who have been saved unto Himself.

You have a soul that is daily engaging the process of being saved by the influence of the word of God and the presence of His Holy Spirit, within you. This is why you find yourself often times in a struggle. A tug of war so to speak, between your regenerated spirit that is influenced by the Holy Spirit and word of God, in battle with the sin nature of your unredeemed flesh *and the eye gates that take in the enticements of the world.*

The challenge to do right or wrong is a choice everyone must make, according to the knowledge which most influences them. God has given all of the tools necessary to make the right decisions, but it requires faith and trust in what He say's, to effectively utilize the tools He's given.

Rom 6:12 Let not sin therefore reign in your mortal body, that ye
    should obey it in the lusts thereof.
Rom 6:13 Neither yield ye your members *as* instruments of
    unrighteousness unto sin: but yield yourselves unto God, as
    those that are alive from the dead, and your members *as*
    instruments of righteousness unto God.

That which is being spoken of now is *holiness.* Redemption is of

Christ. Righteousness is a result of redemption in Christ. Holiness

is a lifestyle that must be pursued by the one who has been

redeemed. Holiness is what God is referring to when it is said to

present your body a living sacrifice, for that is what will be

acceptable to the Lord. Not only would you be presenting

something acceptable to God, but you would have also made the

most intelligent decision anyone could have made, which is to live

a life of holiness. This holiness is a lifestyle in which you must not

only enter into, but you must continue in it by the renewing of

your mind. Because this is the good, acceptable and perfect will of

God. God's will must be proven in the earth by your choice of conduct, and it requires you to be selfless at heart.

Rom 6:16 Know ye not, that to whom ye yield yourselves servants
    to obey, his servants ye are to whom ye obey; whether of sin
    unto death, or of obedience unto righteousness?
Rom 6:17 But God be thanked, that ye were the servants of sin,
    but ye have obeyed from the heart that form of doctrine which
    was delivered you.
Rom 12:1 I beseech you therefore, brethren, by the mercies of
    God, that ye present your bodies a living sacrifice, holy,
    acceptable unto God, *which is* your reasonable service.
Rom 12:2 And be not conformed to this world: but be ye
    transformed by the renewing of your mind, that ye may prove
    what *is* that good, and acceptable, and perfect, will of God.

There are only two options to how we live our lives. The way of

the world, which is influenced by Satan and evil. Or the way of

holiness, which is influenced by God and His word. The knowledge

of and influence of the Word of God, empowers you to disengage

the lust of the flesh, the lust of the eyes and the pride of life. The

selfless aspect of your nature will influence and encourage you to

walk according to how your regenerated spirit is directing you and

in doing so you will not fulfill the lust of the flesh, but the purpose and perfect will of God for your life.

Gal 5:16 *This* I say then, Walk in the spirit, and ye shall not fulfill the lust of the flesh.

The pursuit of this holiness, will settle you in the foundation of holiness as the anchor that secures you in a place to where the way of the world will no longer have an influence in you. Now, the word of instruction given to you by God will have a place to take root. Follow carefully what God is instructing you to do as it relates to marriage.

Know that marriage itself is never the problem. Ignorance is. The good news is that God reveals through His Word, the keys to a perfect marriage. Here, is how those keys are represented. As you will see while reviewing God's instruction to your responsibility in the marriage. These keys to a perfect marriage will be discussed in more detail later in the chapter.

Perfect Marriage

Personal   **M**onogamous

Exclusive   **A**ppreciative

Revealing   **R**ighteous

Fulfilling   **R**elevant

Empowering   **I**ntegral

Credible   **A**uthentic

Total   **G**odly

          Everlasting

➤A husband needs from his wife to be respected➥

A husband needs from his wife to be respected, honored, appreciated, and acknowledged as a leader. These are the most basic and probably the most important needs of a man in the marriage.

Men are very sensitive to the idea of appearing to be weak in any form. So wives I admonish you to make every attempt to overlook his weaknesses in conversation and give more attention to his uniqueness. You will notice that by honing in on his uniqueness and strengths, you will cause the best of his attributes to be influenced, to the point where he himself will begin to give attention to his own weaknesses, and make effort to improve upon them. In addition, acknowledging and understanding the true value of his uniqueness, will even change the way you see him. Your thoughts of him will take on a new direction.

The quality of the man your husband will be is determined mostly by your conduct towards him. Here are a few factors to consider as it relates to your conduct and mindset in the marriage. Remember, you chose "I do", for better or for worse. The purpose of that statement, is to indicate there will be some instances to where you wished you hadn't married.

- ❖ Be committed to your choice of who you married

- ❖ Always be sensitive to and pay close attention to the signals, and if it be necessary change direction from where your emotions are leading you. To avoid any pending disaster that would be imminent.

- ❖ A man wants a woman who is not afraid to show her love for him. Your expressions of that love should begin with your physical appearance. How you present yourself to him.

- ❖ Manipulation is a poison, and should never be used when it comes to sex, to control your husband. The fallout could destroy any possibility of a happy life together.

- ❖ Never allow infatuation or lust to be mistaken for love when having sex. Don't settle for the excitement when there is no true commitment. Love is transparent, and that transparency will keep you in patience, and trust, which can maneuver its' way through any issue that may arise.

❧A wife needs from her husband, (to be his exclusively)❧

A wife needs from her husband, love (to be his exclusively), a protector (from every attack or threat against the family), a provider (of whatever is needed), trust (being transparent in communications and accountable for his actions), intimacy (to be adored, honored and understood), a leader (to be the lead spiritually in everything pertaining to life). These make up the very foundation to having a wife who is complete and confident within the marriage and family relationship. With these foundational pieces in place you will find evidence of the presence of the women that God speaks of in Proverbs:31. She is capable, she is precious, she is trustworthy, she stewards with good things, she is willing in her service to her husband, she rises early to provide for her household, she is savvy with the business of the family, she is strong, she is full of light that is never extinguished, she extends her hand to the poor and needy, she has no fear, her husband is

known amongst the leaders, she speaks with wisdom and loving

instruction, she watches over the household, her children call her

blessed, and her husband praises her. This is the picture of, the

virtuous women who is established in the love and care of a

husband, who treats her as Christ treats the church.

> Eph 5:25 Husbands, love your wives, even as Christ also loved the church, and gave himself for it;
> 1Ti 5:8 But if any provide not for his own, and specially for those of his own house, he hath denied the faith, and is worse than an infidel.

Can a man understand his wife? According to the gainsayers, it's

an impossibility. But according to the word of God, the answer is

yes.

(ISV) 1Pe 3:7 In a similar way, you husbands must live with your
wives in an understanding manner, as with a most delicate
partner. Honor them as heirs with you of the gracious gift of
life, so that nothing may interfere with your prayers.

It is vitally imperative husbands to in patience give very detailed

attention to your wife. Understanding her is only as difficult as you

make it. There are always signs and signals to guide you, whether

they are verbal or implied. You must give attention to knowing

your wife's signals to understand her ways. Be diligent to give

credence to what she places great value on, because it is not in

your best interest to attempt to apply reasoning to a women's

wisdom. That reasoning will usually return to bite you. The

emotions and sensitivity of your wife carry great value when put in

the proper perspective. As the saying goes _"Happy Wife, Happy_

Life", your home will be blessed.

- ❖ Be committed to your choice. The women whom you married will be the wife that you build her up to be.

- ❖ Always be sensitive to and pay close attention to her signals, knowing her thought process and welcoming her emotions will draw her into to you to follow you as you lead her.

- ❖ She will be the women whom is not afraid to show her love for you as you comfort her to establish her confidence and trust in you . Your expressions of that love should be gentleness and kindness toward her.

- ❖ Manipulation is a poison, and should never be used when it comes to sex, to control your wife. Never force yourself on her, but win her over by making yourself available to assist her with the common task of home making, to show how you value and appreciate what she does every day.

❖ Never allow yourself to be driven by lust to simply fulfill your male desires, but rather be taken by her sensuality and beauty that she works tirelessly to put on display for you. Your love making will be off the charts when having sex. Show her that there is true commitment to your love for her. Love is gentle, and that gentleness shows that you care, and it will anchor her trust in you while igniting her passion for you, as she recognizes the love of Christ, in you.

🙠A Perfect Marriage🙢

Personal – in marriage you belong to each other exclusively. You have become one, and your interactions are to be deliberate in serving each other, be it privately or publicly.

Exclusive – you are intended for the sole and purposeful use of one another in love without invasion by foreign entities of any kind.

Revealing – you should disclose and expose the most inner part of who you are, while at the same time discovering more of yourself with your spouse as a helper, to draw it out of you.

Fulfilling – together you will complete each other, satisfying each other's needs and desires, and in that a constant conversion is taking place to create the perfect marriage.

Empowering – you enable, sanction, permit each other to having the full authority to speak into one another's life, and to also make use of each other's body in the fulfillment of the natural need for intimacy and sexual relations. Within the confines of marriage.

Credible – your relationship in view of others lends credibility to the presence of God in your relationship.

Total – your marriage represents the fullness of the Godhead, and the intended purpose behind the creation of man and his representation of God in the kingdom of the earth.

Monogamous – you have each other until death, let there be no separation. Only Christ be present with you in the midst of your marriage relations, especially in intimacy. No other entity has the authority or right to intermingle with your marriage. You are committed to each other for life and throughout life.

Appreciative – you recognize one another's worth and place a very high value upon the life you share as one. You enjoy, admire, cherish, respect, and esteem each other to the highest level possible. Thereby causing one another to improve, daily rising to the occasion of fulfilling God's intended purpose for marriage.

Righteous – your attitude towards one another is ethical and chaste, honorable with good intention to impart a noble virtue to the building up of the character in your marriage.

Relevant – the energy you give to one another is germane in the way to which you uphold the truth in what God created and intended marriage to be, between one man and one women.

Integral – you are made up of two essential parts yet not separate from the other, to form a single unit. Each, being an indispensable part of a whole which is formed to represent a unity, even as God the Father, Son, and Holy Spirit are one. So are you in unity together with Him by the same Holy Spirit.

Authentic – your marriage is real, true, genuine, and pure, comprised of the accurate, reliable, legitimate, and factual creative power of God by His word.

Godly – you are saints, made pure by Christ divine redemption. You are made righteous in Him and by His Spirit you live holy together and before God and man, in representation of the Heavenly Godhead.

Everlasting – your marriage is to be permanent, ceaseless, and endless, continuing throughout your time spent alive here on this earth. From that you together with the church will unite with Christ in marriage throughout eternity. Which, is **"The Perfect Marriage".**

Chapter IX

Self Relationships (Monologist)
Representing a prolonged talk or discourse by a single speaker monopolizing a conversation

At the very beginning of this book, it was mentioned in the authors commentary that mankind was created in the image and likeness of God. In considering that statement of truth, this book would be incomplete without the mention and examination of what could be suggested to represent, what might be God's most impressive attribute as it relates to the God way of doing, as His creation of mankind.

From the very beginning of God's word in Genesis, His ability to monologue, having a proactive conversation with Himself, prior to the manifested realities of His creation, was and is the absolute order of how God did everything. These conversations would commence with words such as, let us, or let there, followed with very precise and detailed instruction, as if to be speaking to another person who would then execute what was spoken. In fact, God established clearly that the Godhead is indeed comprised of three distinct personalities embodied within a single being. Each personality has a specific characteristic which authenticates His position and authority in the godhead and creation. God the father has never, throughout all creation, created anything without first communing with His Son, the Christ (Jesus) and the Holy Spirit. In everything that has been created, their corporate influence is clearly evident.

God said to Himself, let us make man in our image and likeness. With that declaration, God included every attribute that formed His image and likeness. Mankind was given them all, including the free will to use them as he pleased, with the expectation that they would be used to reflect God's image and likeness, within mans kingdom the earth. Thereby putting on display "The Power of Self".

The problem we have in the world today, as it relates to mankind displaying the image and likeness of God, is that mankind has lost the ability to harness, benefit or even comprehend his own God given attributes. For mankind to even consider that he is anything like God is simply ludicrous, without him first renewing his mind, through God's word, enabling him to think of himself in a totally different light. Which is the image and likeness of God.

You are probably thinking, why is it that people don't have the ability to see themselves the way that God created them.

There is two ways to answer such a question. One answer is, man does still have access to the ability to see himself as God created him, in God's image and likeness. The other answer is, because man relinquished the ability to comprehend that he is like God, when Adam, the first man allowed deception and selfish desires to rob him of His fellowship with God, along with the awareness that he was like God. Mankind giving in to deception and selfish desire, caused sin to enter mans kingdom of the earth. This sin consumed the nature of man and not only cut off his fellowship with God, but also his awareness of God, in addition to his awareness of being godlike. His awareness of God and him being like God, began to slowly diminish with each day of his life. So mankind became more distant and more devoid of God's existence. Hopelessly spiraling into a deep web of self sufficiency, which end is a life of emptiness and being unfulfilled, in having any purpose in life.

The reason this is such a big deal, is because mankind was created for fellowship. Fellowship with God, and fellowship with his fellow man. This fellowship begins within ones self, the very same way God interacts and fellowships within Himself. God has set a distinctive order in the way that things are to be done, both in the spirit realm and in the natural realm where mankind is supposed to have dominion. But, purpose escaped mans concept of being purposeful, when he no longer had anything to have dominion over.

Instead of dialog within ones self through the process of monologue, to determine what is right and good. Man engaged in dialog with creations adversary, the devil. Prior to this external dialog, the devil had no authority in man's earth kingdom.

Dominion was given to him by man, when mankind yielded to the deception, and forfeited his identity. But God refused to leave mankind in exile without identity of his true likeness and purpose. God provided mankind with a hope of rediscovering his true identity and value in creation.

There is only one possible way of reclaiming his identity, purpose, and true value. It is through redemption by Christ Jesus, and the renewing of ones mind through God's word (the Bible).

Maturing in the process of renewing of ones mind through God's word, requires the activity of a monologue. That is, engaging in interactive dialog with ones self, in spirit, soul, and body, relative to the truth and reality of God's word, and the application of it in a sin ridden world. Engaging in this prescribed type of behavior, is where man now begins to once again reflect the image and likeness of God, his creator. Through maturity, by faith is how the activity of a man putting on display, his image and likeness of God, by having reclaimed his true identity and value in creation is accomplished. Please acknowledge, understand, and accept the fact, that mankind is the only created being in God's entire creation, that has been given God's very image and likeness, with God's corresponding attributes..

❧Testimonials❧

Eric & Susan (*God's plan was always for us to love one another*)

Well, here is how we will begin our testimony of how we were finally brought together in Christ.

I met my wife after a long bout with struggles of the world, as I found myself having to care for a baby girl with no mother to help me care for her. I dove into a depressed state and began to self medicate myself. During that time it was all about me. Then I was introduced to this single mother, or so I thought she was, but she was going through a separation with two children of her own. We were both self medicating, and it was all about doing things that made us happy. We were not concerned about much of anything else. But somehow the children and the bills were always taken care of. But still our homes were not as they should have been.

To get to the main point directly, we eventually hit bottom, and separated from each other, after a long and destructive relationship. This happened after we had gotten married. Our marriage was not a union from the Lord, but of our own doing. So nothing went right for us from that point. That is until we began to accept some spiritual guidance from loved ones, and gave it a go. The selfish and destructive lifestyle was out and our life was now on its way to a much better and more fulfilled life together, serving the Lord. We are now actively involved in our church and unselfishly giving of ourselves. Knowing this, that God's plan was always for us to love one another. Praise the Lord!

Connie and Grady
(a testimony of my selfless love in memory of my only true love)

I met Grady July 8th 2011 at the Omaha summer jazz fest. Grady
Wilkins was the music director for "The Whispers", a singing group
that I always loved. I thank God, that I have always had a secret
crush on the twins Walter and Scotty, or I would not have ever
met my soul mate.

From the first night we met he changed my world, because I lived
in Omaha Nebraska for 28 years and never thought I would ever
leave. Grady and I would always have debates on who God was
listening to most, because Grady said God brought me to him, and
I would say no, I asked God to bring him to me.

Our relationship became very serious, after knowing each other
for only five months. He would say from the start, you are my
wife, and that we were going to be together.

I thought he was crazy, however all of the events that brought us together did seem a bit strange. I decided to take a chance on him, and I have no regrets. We both needed something from each other, so we talked a lot, and we learned so much about each other. After being together for only a short time, he found out he had cancer, and it was so devastating. But we decided together that we would just go with the flow.

I remember the very day he called me from the hospital. He called me immediately, after he found out the doctor's had done all that they could. I was numb, but somehow found the strength to get on a plane and go to him. I thought this is not real, but I knew that we would get thru it somehow. Grady and I both had been married before, but this was the first time that we experienced what true love really felt like. I was so grateful, that before he got really sick, we had learned so much about what it takes to be in a love relationship that was unconditional.

We were from two completely different worlds, yet we had so much in common. We laughed about the fact that I would say, if I had met you years ago, I would not have liked you. But because of all we had been thru in prior relationships, and with life's up's and downs. Our relationship was so good, and our love for each other was so real. I chose to leave my comfort zone, to be with him. Because I was never one who did anything spontaneously, or take risk to exploring the unknown, everyone thought I was crazy. My family, and my friends, but I did not care.

We were married the first year we met, but we did not have a formal ceremony. so when it was confirmed that he might not make it. We decided to have a spiritual wedding ceremony. It was more beautiful than any big wedding could have ever been.

Several people asked me, why did I marry him, if you knew he was dying. It certainly was not for his money, because he didn't have much. Yes, my husband had a very successful career in music, and if he had made better choices, he would have been very rich, however the entertainment world can make you do stupid things. Grady was lost, and lived a reckless life. He really didn't know who he was, nor who the people in his life were. Whether they loved him for him, or what he did.

Grady did know that my love for him was genuine. I never cared that he did not have the finances, because he was rich in other ways, more valuable than material things. He would make me angry, after he was admitted to hospice. He would always say things like, I am sorry because this was not the life that I wanted for you. Then he would thank me for everything I did. I'd tell him that he should not feel like he had to say thank you, because I was doing the things that was I suppose to do.

Sometimes I think about my life, how I moved from Omaha, to Las Vegas, and from Las Vegas, to California. I never considered my own health, having multiple sclerosis. I was more concerned about making him happy. I know, he wanted so much to give me everything I ever said I wanted, and he was working on doing just that, thru his music. It's funny he use to tell me when we first met, he wanted to be in love with someone he loved more than they could ever love him. I did not understand that, until after he had passed. I truly loved him for who he was, not for what he was. He taught me so much about life, as I did him. I believe that because we had God in our life, it made all the difference. We did not go to church every Sunday, because his career made it difficult to do so. We did however make time to have our own spiritual connection with God as time allowed. I realized being with him, that there is a big difference in loving someone, and being in love with someone. With Grady, I discovered that I was in love for the first time in my life, and I believe he was too. I don't know if I will ever feel for someone else the way I felt and today, still feel about Grady. What makes me feel good about our relationship, is the fact that even though we were together for a short period of time, I was told by his friends, and family, that they had never witnessed him so happy, as he was with me.

In the last weeks before he passed, I would read scriptures from the bible or read inspirational books to him, so before he died, he was really at peace. He also was able to forgive himself, as well as others. Once Grady got angry and expressed that he wanted to end our relationship. I felt he wanted to run like he had always done in past relationships. I said to him, what ever you want to do is ok with me, and with that I thanked him for making me happy, and I felt no regrets at all, and said that I will always love him. His closes friends would call me to say don't walk away, because he always does this when he is scared. I felt in part that he was protecting me from suffering through the illness with him.

When his father passed away, we talked a about their relationship. Grady called me to ask me if I would come to be with him for his fathers funeral. Afterwards we really discussed things that were not right in our relationships, past situations that caused problems. From that we decided that from now on, our past is in the past. We then wrote down our problems and burned the paper, never looking back. So sad that death brought us back together, even though it was only a break up of two weeks. I knew he couldn't live without me, Ha Ha.

The day he died, I had just return from Las Vegas. I was taking our dog Nina to a friends, who dog sit her for us, until we could find our own place. I did not understand why he wanted me to fly there then turn around and come right back. But I am so glad that

I did. I remember entering our house, hearing his voice saying, is that my wife? He really enjoyed saying, you are my wife. We had some good laughs and conversation. It had been a beautiful day. I had left him for only about fifteen minutes, and when I returned and entered our room, Grady was already gone. The beautiful thing is that he had a smile on his face when he passed. He had made peace with himself, and with God. He was ready to go. He sometimes would think that he was a burden to me. I never felt that way, and would have done anything for him. I know, that if he had to, he would have done the same. People are amazed at how I handle my loss, I know he is in a better place, so his spirit gives me the strength to go on and to finish the things he started musically. My most favorite song ever, is "What you won't do for love", by Bobby Caldwell. I loved this song for years, because of the lyrics. Now, I truly understand when you love someone with all your heart, there is nothing you won't do for love.

There is a song I love dearly. Grady wrote a song for me called, "I can Smile", and every time I listen to it, in the mornings, or when I am feeling sad,"I can smile". People come into your life for a reason, a season and for a lifetime. Grady is and will always be my lifetime love, forever, until we meet again.

❧Reflections❧

This manuscript was written for your reading pleasure and as a source of information for your consideration. I exhort you to give very serious consideration to the power you have within yourself, and what affect your life has had, and even does now have on your home, your spouse, your children, your family, your community and even the world. Consider truly, even that God created you in His very image and His own likeness. Consider that you are as He is, manifested in a body of flesh. His Spirit, embodied within the heart of your spirit. Consider His love for His creation and for His children, and with that consideration that you would be all that He is within you. That my friend, would be your true value in the earth. That you, will allow the fullness of God to live in and through you in the earth. Take it and only exchange it for your heavenly reward, which is to hear Him say, well done, My good and faithful servant.

Please consider yourself to be workers with Him, as represented by this poetic presentation of who God created you to be:

"THE MIRROR"

Just in passing, I looked in the mirror a

short distance away

As I continued to look the image drew me closer to see

An image that appeared to look so much like

me

The closer I got, and the more I looked,

The image began to change

For what I saw, or thought was me, began to

look more like eternity

As I drew closer, this appeared to me, more

and more strange

Because the image I thought was me,

continuously began to change

Suddenly as I looked deeper, I couldn't see

me any more

I was being drawn into something so vast and

So deep, and as I finally reached its inner core

A voice spoke to me gently, saying, come in,

there is more

As I journeyed in deeper into this image,

that I thought I knew

The voice of the image began to mold me, and

shape me, into something I knew no more

I had no control, and only then I realized,

I was no longer my own

For the image that I looked into, and

thought it was just me

Was the image of My Creator, making an image

of Himself to see

This all began to overwhelm me, for the

face that I had known

Was now the face of My Lord and Creator God,

sitting high upon His Throne?

It is an awesome miracle to see, how My

Creator God, chose me,

To reflect an image of Himself to see

So I am locked inside this mirror of endless

time and space, watching joyfully,

My Lord smiling, at the reflection of His face

by: Gary L. Wilkerson
© August 2007

For bookings; call (424) 253-6303 or

email; gods1general@gmail.com, garywilkerson@gileadsprings.org

The most important key to reclaiming your true value is

SUBMITTING;

<u>S</u>elfless – *the denial of your own personal and private motives*

<u>U</u>nified – *to be in agreement with another*

<u>B</u>eliefs – *spiritual and moral concepts of life*

<u>M</u>anifesting – *daily growth and development of life in relation to another, benefiting all*

<u>I</u>ntimate – *open hearted, personal and private love, affection and caring of another*

<u>T</u>rust – *dedicated confidence, dependance and faith in another*

<u>T</u>hat – *the action leading to, or assisting with*

<u>I</u>mplements – *the tool used to fulfill or carryout the action of being*

<u>N</u>ourished – *delivery of nutriment needed for growth and life*

<u>G</u>rowth – *an absolute gradual increase, the process of growing*

If you have found that this book has enlightened you and has given you hope for a brighter future. But there may be some things that do not make sense to you or doesn't seem to apply to you because you don't have the relationship with God that it speaks of. Don't lose heart, God has made a way for you to encounter and enjoy the relational benefits that are mentioned in what you have just read.

God's word gives very simple instructions to how you too can have a personal relationship with Him, and successful relationships with everyone you encounter throughout your entire life.

Here is what Jesus said about His purpose for coming to the earth.

(ISV) Joh 3:16 "For this is how God loved the world: He gave his unique Son so that everyone who believes in him might not be lost but have eternal life.

Here is how you can receive eternal life.

(ISV) Rom 10:9 If you declare with your mouth that Jesus is Lord, and believe in your heart that God raised him from the dead, you will be saved.

Rom 10:10 For one believes with his heart and is justified, and declares with his mouth and is saved.

Rom 10:11 **The Scripture says, "Everyone who believes in him will never be ashamed."**

❧You have just reclaimed your true value☙

Made in the USA
Charleston, SC
08 October 2015